Stepping Stones

Meditations in a Garden

by

LILLIAN MARSHALL

PETER PAUPER PRESS, INC.
White Plains ● New York

INTRODUCTION

Once, walking through a lovely garden deep in thought, the scene before me suddenly became obscured by a silvery, golden mist through which a rise of wide, shimmering steps appeared, seven planes of rainbow radiant hues reaching to the sky. I stopped amazed, entranced. "Seven steps," I breathed in awe.

"Yes. Seven steps," a voice seemed to speak aloud, then fading, "to reach the heights - of spiritual consciousness."

It ended silent as a thought. The vision silvered and faded with it. The memory has never faded. It seemed an answer to my seeking at the time in spiritual readings. What step or steps I have attained in the years since, I do not know.

I only know that putting one's hand in the Hand of God and going forward, giving thought each day to His Presence, one rises in faith, strength and understanding, and His guidance leads to light through troubled times. A quiet time each day affirming His nearness keeps one on a rising path.

Through the years I have made notes of guiding thoughts that have come to me in meditations and this little book is a gleaning of them.

Envision each flower illustration in this slim volume aglow with the life and beauty the Creator gave it, release the thought of the meditation to the ear of God, and feel the all-pervading Life. Love, Truth, a radiant light of divine action within you, around you, bringing it into being.

May each page bless to a healing and higher consciousness. A rising to higher planes of eternal Truth.

L.M.

Prayer is the proclamation of
A joyful and beholding soul.
                    Emerson

More things are wrought by prayer
Than this world dreams of . . . .
For so the whole round earth is every way
Bound by gold chains about the feet of God.
                    Tennyson

And so I find it well to come
For deeper rest to this still room
For here the habit of the soul
Feels less the outer world's control
And from the silence multiplied
By these still forms on every side
The world that time and sense has known
Falls off and leaves us, God, alone.
                    Whittier

You may not choose to follow my light
But if I have a light I should offer it to you.
                    Unknown

FAITH

Stepping Stones

**Meditations in
a Garden**

It is through quiet, spiritual meditation that we reach into that Divine Presence dwelling in the center of our heart and pervading the Universe.

Believing this we are assured that God can restore us and sustain us.

And we need only to trust and accept His Divine Guidance in our lives.

7

Within you is the secret place where God speaks when you call upon Him in the silence of your prayer, a place of peace and joy in the spirit, the center of radiating health in your body.

Peace and joy go before you as you turn to the call of life's duties and activities and all is well.

Advancing begins with the first step forward. Whither shall your feet go? What road shall you follow?

Put your hand in the Hand of God and listen to His voice direct you. With faith in His wisdom and guidance go forth with confidence and walk into your good.

STRENGTH

Resting assured in God's perfect, ever-present love casts out all fear and doubt. He guides your life into freedom and security.

His love is a light shining down upon you, pervading you and radiating from you.

His love is a circle of guidance and protection that glows around you.

Let joy fill your soul and radiate around you. Hold the inner light of love shining within.

Sadness or depression cannot last when Faith and Joy and Love flood the mind.

Feel Gladness and Inspiration in your spirit's attunement with God.

Friendship is a giving and a receiving, a sharing of companionship blessed by the Supreme Spirit of caring for another.

Love, laughter and joy fill friendship with comfort and the Blessing of God.

Give of your friendship and friendship will return to you manifold.

You are never alone. God is always with you. His companionship enfolds you.

Feel it, admit it, and know that wherever you are, wherever you go, the loving and protective presence of God is with you.

Rely on this presence and it brings harmonious companionship your way.

11

The essence of spiritual healing is a conviction that God's will of perfection is a within and encircling presence.

The spirit of Perfect Life fills you with health and joy.

Daily welcome and absorb this faith and your life becomes happy, healthy and complete.

Enjoy today. Dissolve the negatives and the cares and troubles of yesterday. Brush out the fears of tomorrow.

Each day is a step into the future conditioned by present acceptance of good.

Live today believing with strong faith that God is in His heaven. The kingdom of heaven is within you, and all is well with your soul and your life.

J   O   Y

Night is the time when the body Rests and the soul Meditates.

At night, before sleep, forgive everything, everyone, even yourself.

Go back over the day and bless the good, dissolve the errors,

Clear the day and expect a good day on the morrow.

True strength glows in the peacemaker. One may take a lonely path but it leads to heaven. In God's presence evil loses Power.

Realizing God's presence in any situation, harmony prevails and discord fades away.

Feel the Divine Presence in all your relationships, and emergencies, and send forth blessings of Peace.

Troubles of mind and pain of body are human experience, shadows obscuring God's plan of joy and health. Bring in light and dissolve the shadows by asserting your faith in God's gift of health and joy.

"My life is from God. God created me, and God sustains me. Life flows through me from the center of Life and carries healing to all my body.

My spirit welcomes and accepts with gratitude the thrill of new strength and renewed health within me."

Hold to this Truth.

Though clouds may seem to obscure it, the sun is always shining.

So do the shadows of my thinking only hide the light of God's presence.

The light of His love is always shining to sweep my clouds away.

Whence cometh the dawn but in the Turning of the earth?

15

God is Spirit, the mystical presence that pervades and directs the Universe, the wellspring of life and love at the center of your being.

Nearer is He than breathing, closer than hands and feet.

Life, Love, Truth, Wisdom pervade your being and surround you.

Each one of us is a directional point of Divine experience.

God sees through your eyes, hears through your ears, feels through your touch.

Become aware of the beauty and harmony in His creation and life becomes filled with loveliness and joy.

The voice of God is silent music in the soul.

Feel love and harmony within you, and love and harmony will pervade all your surroundings.

S P I R I T

The most menial task is a contribution to Universal good. Feel the presence of God and His approval in whatever work you are called upon to do.

Life is progression and good deeds lead upwards.

Joy and devotion in the present duties beautifies the work and leads to expanding trusts and attainments.

Trust in the ever-presence of God, the Supreme Creative Being of the Universe.

Hope keeps the receptive faculty of your mind ever open to His direction.

His direction is to your good.

It is His good pleasure to give you the kingdom of joy, success, completion.

Forgiveness is a release from bondage to a wrong idea. Today forgive yourself for mistakes you have made.

Forgive all others who have seemingly erred against you.

Thus does God forgive and you are freed into joy and comforted in love.

When we see the good in others and think of them with love, gratitude and understanding, only good can come from them to us. We are all One in the Presence of God.

Forgiveness is Divine. It frees the spirit and relaxes the emotions so that love and joy can rush in.

Forgive and see the presence of God in any inharmonious relationship, and feel the release of God's forgiveness within yourself.

Feel healed of all disharmony physically and mentally, and your heart is filled with joy. Let peace go forth from you and feel it return to you radiantly.

*Life does not end with death and
therefore that love being life's soul
must endure forever.*
Papyrus Areana BC 1300

Grieve not for the one who made
the test of life and has advanced to
higher realms of universal mansions
of the soul.

Love is a link into the unseen and
when across the shore, free of earth's
boundaries you meet again, love will be
enriched for evermore.

Do you fear something or someone?
Dislike something or someone?
Fear meeting some person or situation?

See it as a passing picture. Build a
picture of the ideal person or the ideal
situation. See it vividly and go forth
with confidence that God is with you.

With faith that God is with you and
whatever you meet, there is no room for
fear. Only harmony will greet you.

H O P E

All life is progression. There is no dead end in living.

Set your direction on the road toward good and watch for God's signs for the right turnings. Worry blocks the spirit from a confident approach to a clear road.

Do not worry about the decisions to make. When made in good faith they will turn out to be right.

Today is a new day that God has given. Faith that today all day He is with you will fill your heart with joy and strength.

Rejoice and feel His love and guidance in all you do.

Bless each task and know that how humble seeming or how hard, it is a creation of good at that part of doing.

Where darkness seems to be see a light. Even a small light dispels the dark in the reach of its radiance.

Light catches the glow of God's presence in the problem and darkness fades away.

Feel encircled and free in the Divine Light.

Each day is a stepping stone into future days on the upward path. Enrich each day with gratitude and a time of quiet.

Rest in the peace of God's presence and feel His love and wisdom and guidance directing you to increasing love, joy and accomplishment.

Today is a day that God has given. Rejoice and be joyful in it.

Plant a seed of love in the dark situation that troubles you and nurture it into a beauty that dispels the darkness and fills your heart with joy.

Let it radiate from you.

God's wise direction guides and surrounds you.

God is Love.

Meet your contingencies with confidence and find joy in their solution.

Each overcoming is a stepping stone in experience. Experience is a necessary ingredient of growth.

Lift your spirit in confidence that God's will for your accomplishment and victory is omnipresent and omnipotent now.

B E A U T Y

God is Omnipotence, ever present, all knowing.

This power strengthens your faith, gives inspiration, and guidance in life's experience and duties with others.

Go forth in the strength and confidence of the God Power that directs you.

A helping hand held out to one in need releases a wellspring of joy that praises God and blesses all.

Good offered to others like seeds in a garden brings forth a flowering of growing good and gratifies the Cosmic Soul.

The inner power of life within you is God. He removes all fear from you.

Hear His voice telling you His will for your good.

Listen and move forward to His guidance and the way opens up to your vast abundant good.

An inner light shines forth and lights your footsteps.

His life flows through you
And truly all shadows that trouble you dissolve and you are free.

Joy in the spirit that is warmed by love.

Is like sunshine dancing on the ripples of sparkling water.

God's love is Joy and dissolves everything unlike itself.

Rest your weariness in the
peace and quiet of the presence of God
which pervades your being and is all
around you.

A moment of quiet closing out all but
the consciousness of His Spirit, and
you are renewed. Now that which you
have a duty to do seems easy and joyous.

And you bless the doing of it to
The All Good.

Peace is the cessation of striving,
the stillness of confidence in God's
loving care.

Peace within is the inner spirit of
Truth, Love, Wisdom.

Let the inner light of Peace illuminate
the way, make beautiful the path ahead
with rainbow colours of divine beauty.

Embrace the glory of the upward path
and rise to the potential within you.

P E A C E

May all blessings of health,
joy, love and prosperity
be with you always
from this day forth
and evermore.

SELAH